IT'LL NEVER WORK

CARS,
TRUCKS AND TRAINS

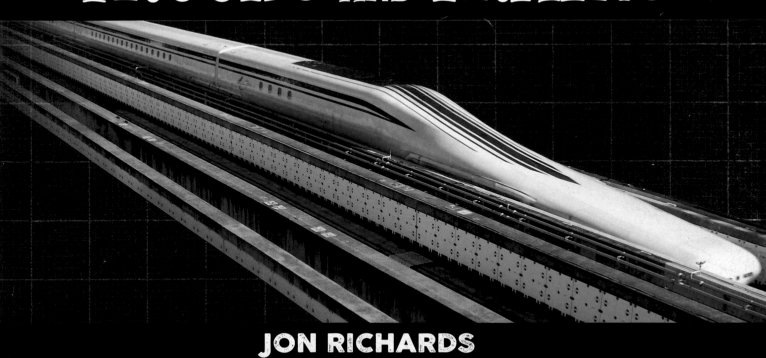

JON RICHARDS

Franklin Watts
First published in Great Britain in 2016 by
The Watts Publishing Group

Copyright © The Watts Publishing
Group, 2016

Conceived, designed and edited by
Tall Tree Ltd
Series Editor: David John
Series Designer: Jonathan Vipond

ISBN 978 1 4451 5022 2

Printed in China

Franklin Watts
An imprint of
Hachette Children's Group
Part of The Watts Publishing Group
Carmelite House
50 Victoria Embankment
London EC4Y 0DZ

An Hachette UK Company
www.hachette.co.uk

www.franklinwatts.co.uk

Picture credits:
t-top, b-bottom, l-left, r-right, c-centre
All images public domain unless otherwise indicated:
Front cover bl, 18br and 31br Dreamstime.
com/28050797, front cover cr and 25br Dreamstime.
com/James Menges, back cover tl and 6-7c Dreamstime.
com/Grace0612, 5tl Utah State Historical Society, 5cr
Dreamstime.com/Bratty1206, 6bl Bundesarchiv, 8bl
GM Heritage Center, 10cr Dreamstime.com/
Robwilson39, 10bl Dreamstime.com/Jarretera, 11t
Library of Congress, 11cr Dreamstime.com/Bankerwin,
11bl Dreamstime.com/Artzzz, 11br Dreamstime.com/
Steve Allen, 12cl Dreamstime.com/Dmitry Kalinovsky,
12bc Dreamstime.com/Sherman2013, 12-13b NHTSA/
DOT, 13tl Dreamstime.com/Otnaydur, 13cr
Dreamstime.com/Hupeng, 15t Flock and Siemens,
16-17b Dreamstime.com/Mlan61, 17cr
WereSpielChequers, 18cr Dreamstime.com/Ilfede, 19tr
Dreamstime.com/Mikhail Starodubov, 19b Dreamstime.
com/Duncan Noakes, 22b Dreamstime.com/Darryl
Brooks, 25c Dreamstime.com/Georgesixth, 29t Spacex

CONTENTS

✹ CHANGING ✹ CARS

Since the invention of the motor car, the shape of what we drive has changed in response to fashion and advances in technology.

THE MOTOR CAR

In 1879, German engineer Karl Benz patented an idea for an internal combustion engine. Using this new power source, he built the first practical, petrol-powered car, called a Motorwagen, in 1885.

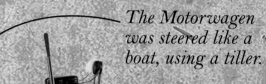

The Motorwagen was steered like a boat, using a tiller.

FOUR-STROKE CYCLE

A modern internal combustion car engine uses a four-stroke cycle to produce power.

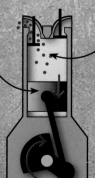

Piston

Fuel and air

First stroke: the piston moves down and air and fuel enter the cylinder.

Second stroke: the piston moves up, squeezing and mixing the air and fuel.

Spark plug

Third stroke: when the piston reaches the top of the cylinder, the spark plug ignites, setting the air and fuel alight and this explosion pushes the piston down

This Ford Model T dates from 1910.

CHEAP CARS

In the USA, Henry Ford revolutionised the car world when he introduced mass-production techniques at his car factory in 1908. Cars were put together on an assembly line, which made them cheaper to produce. Before then, cars had been a luxury, but now they were affordable.

FRESH IDEAS

The Mini was a British car made from 1959 to 2000. Its low cost and small size proved hugely popular. The Mini's innovations included a front-wheel-drive engine that freed up 80 per cent of the car's tiny size for passengers and luggage.

This model of the Mini was launched in 1960.

5

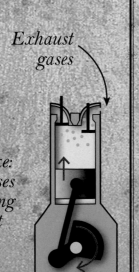
Exhaust gases

Fourth stroke: the piston rises again, pushing the exhaust gases out.

Google

✹ ELECTRIC ✹ CARS

While Karl Benz was inventing the internal combustion engine, others were making electric motors. In the early part of the twentieth century, electric cars were more popular than petrol cars.

EARLY ELECTRIC

The first practical electric car was built by English engineer Thomas Parker in 1884. It had a top speed of just 30 kilometres per hour, but it made no fumes and was perfect for driving in cities. By the 1890s, fleets of electric cabs hummed along the streets of Europe's capitals.

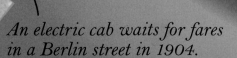

An electric cab waits for fares in a Berlin street in 1904.

CELL POWER

A fuel cell produces electricity from a chemical reaction. The fuel cell has three parts – an anode, an electrolyte and a cathode. As hydrogen enters the anode it is split into a hydrogen ion and an electron. The ion can pass through the electrolyte, but the electron cannot – it has to pass through a wire, and this produces an electric current that is used to power the car. The ion and the electron join back together at the cathode and they react with oxygen to produce water.

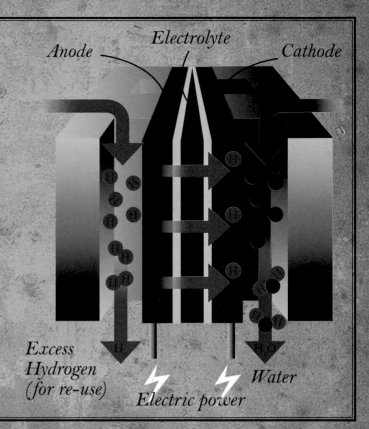

Anode

Electrolyte

Cathode

Excess Hydrogen (for re-use)

Electric power

Water

SUN POWER

With cheap energy from the Sun, running a solar-powered car should be a no-brainer. It costs just 15 pence per 100 km to run a solar-powered car, compared to £10 for a petrol-driven car. At the moment, however, the number of solar cells that can be fitted on a car can only produce the same power used in a toaster – so they are only used to drive small, one-person vehicles, but the technology continues to improve.

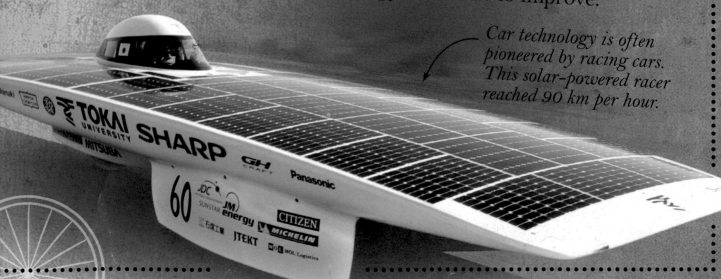

Car technology is often pioneered by racing cars. This solar-powered racer reached 90 km per hour.

CAR DESIGN

Since they first appeared at the end of the nineteenth century, cars have changed shape in response to changes in technology, tastes and fashions, and how they are used.

'BOXY' CARS

Many cars of the 1920s and 1930s still retained the carriage-like body shape of horse-drawn transport, including the running boards along the sides. They were boxy and not aerodynamically designed for speed.

A Rolls Royce 1937 Sedanca Deville.

10

A Volkswagen Beetle

FAMILY CARS

Introduced in wartime Germany in 1941, the Volkswagen (meaning 'people's car') was designed to be a cheap car for the masses. Production soared after the war, and by 1992, more than 21 million had been produced worldwide. Since then, family cars have remained popular and come in a variety of shapes and sizes, including estate cars which have a large boot space to the rear.

A Bantam jeep jumping into the air in tests in North Carolina, in 1941.

This Range Rover Evoque was designed as a luxury off-road vehicle.

OFF-ROAD

The earliest off-road vehicles were designed for the military. One of the first was the jeep used by Allied forces during the Second World War (1939–45). Off-road vehicles became popular with the public after the war, and today, some models have developed into luxury cars, such as Range Rover.

HYPERCARS

High-performance cars such as the Bugatti Veyron (below) push car design to the cutting edge. For example, the Veyron has composite disc brakes to slow it from very high speeds.

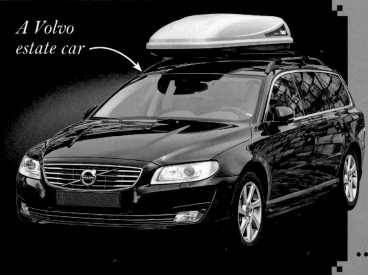

A Volvo estate car

SAFETY
FEATURES

Early cars were dangerous things to be in. Steering columns could stick into the driver and dashboards were hard with sharp edges.

CAR DANGERS

About 20 million people around the world have been killed in crashes on poor roads, or with pedestrians or other vehicles. Over the years, car engineers and road designers have created many features that help to make driving safer.

SEAT BELTS

The first patent for a safety belt was granted in 1885. Early belts were simple straps that fixed across the lap. Carmakers now fit vehicles with three-point seat belts, which have straps across the lap and body to spread the energy from a crash. In the USA alone, it is estimated that safety belts save 15,000 lives every year.

AIRBAGS 👉

Airbags were first introduced in the mid-1970s and are designed to inflate quickly and then deflate during a crash, protecting car users from hitting the steering wheel, dashboard and side pillars in a car. The first designs used compressed air, but this couldn't inflate the bags quickly enough, and today nitrogen gases are used to fully fill the bags in less than 80 milliseconds.

👈 DUMMIES

To see if safety features work, car designers use test dummies. In fact, the first test dummies were dead bodies! However, these could only provide limited data, so dummies were used instead. Today's dummies have sensors to collect and record information about crashes in many different situations.

✸ THE NEED ✸ FOR SPEED

Since the first cars were built, car manufacturers have tried to push them faster and faster, creating new engines and revolutionary designs.

La Jamais Contente *set the land speed record in 1899 with a top speed of 105.882 kph.*

👉 1. STEAM AND ELECTRIC

The earliest land speed records were set by electric and steam-powered cars. One of the earliest was the French electric car *La Jamais Contente*, which had a torpedo-shaped body to make it more streamlined.

JETS AND ROCKETS 👉

Internal combustion engines could only push cars so fast. More powerful sources were needed if cars were to go faster, so designers turned to rocket science. In 1970, US racing driver Gary Gabelich drove the rocket-powered *Blue Flame* to a staggering 1,014.656 kph. It held the land speed record for 13 years.

The Blue Flame's *dart shape made it extremely aerodynamic.*

Bloodhound SSC *is designed to travel faster than 1,600 kph.*

FASTER THAN SOUND 👉

Bloodhound SSC is being built to break the land speed record of 1,228 kph. It will use both jets and rockets to blast it beyond the speed of sound. Everything on this car is designed and tested to withstand extremes. Normal wheels would simply disintegrate at such speeds, so *Bloodhound* will run on solid wheels. These are specially shaped to within thousandths of a millimetre and made from a tough alloy of aluminium and zinc.

FORMULA ONE

Formula One racing teams spend millions of pounds every year trying to make their cars go faster. While many ideas don't get off the ground, some do make it onto the track. One of these was the Tyrrell P34 from 1976, which used six wheels, rather than four. It won a race, but it soon proved too heavy and uncompetitive, so it was abandoned.

The Tyrrell P34 with four front wheels.

A modern Formula One car.

TRUCKS

Trucks are vehicles that are designed to carry cargo. They vary in size depending on what they have to carry and where they have to travel.

EARLY TRUCKS

The world's first powered vehicle was actually built a century before the car. In 1771, French engineer Nicolas-Joseph Cugnot designed a steam-driven truck. It was heavy, hard to control and soon crashed into a wall. Other early trucks were hampered by poor roads, which kept the trucks small and their cargo light.

Here, Cugnot struggles to steer his vehicle and collides with a wall in the world's first vehicle crash.

A nineteenth-century steam wagon like this one would have carried dry goods.

Flat bed

A Second World War DUKW

PICKUP TRUCKS

The first pickup trucks were modified cars, such as the Ford Model T (see page 5), fitted with a flat bed on the back to carry cargo. Soon specialist models were developed with greater comfort in the cab. Today, more pickup trucks in the USA are used for recreation than as work vehicles.

Cab

17

Pickup trucks are known as 'utes' (short for 'utility vehicles') in Australia and New Zealand.

MASSIVE TRUCKS

Today, massive trucks carry enormous loads over vast distances, and they come in a wide range of shapes and designs.

CONTAINER TRUCKS 👉

Articulated trucks feature a tractor unit that pulls a trailer. The join between the two parts can bend, allowing the truck to turn corners. The trailer on a container truck is designed to carry a standard shipping container from a dockyard to its destination.

Tractor unit

Trailer

An articulated truck leaves a dock with a cargo container on its trailer.

18

ROAD TRAINS

A road train with three trailers.

Improvements in the quality of roads, including the invention of tarmac to create a smooth surface, and the development of more powerful engines have seen trucks increase in size and strength. Road trains are some of the longest trucks in the world. These giants pull three and some times four trailers across Australia.

TRUCK CRANES

Mobile truck cranes have an extendible arm, called a boom, which stretches high into the air to lift loads into hard-to-reach locations. Larger truck cranes have multiple wheels to provide a solid base while lifting and many also have extendible stabilisers to stop the crane from tipping.

With its stabilisers out, this truck has been able to extend its crane to lift supplies onto a building site.

TIPPER TRUCKS

Working in mining and quarrying involves moving heavy loads of rock and sand. The huge trucks involved in this work are fitted with a large hopper, which they can tip up to pour out their load. Other types of truck, such as garbage trucks, also have hoppers.

This tipper truck has raised its hopper to dump its load.

19

⚙ STEAM ⚙
LOCOMOTIVES

Although people had known about the power of steam to move objects and drive machines for thousands of years, it wasn't until the nineteenth century that the first successful steam-powered trains appeared.

EARLY RAIL 👉

The first rail vehicles were pulled or pushed by animals and even people. At the start of the 1800s, English inventor and engineer Richard Trevithick built the world's first steam locomotive. However, there were many failed experiments and models before he got things right, including the London Steam Carriage (1803), a horseless carriage which proved more uncomfortable and expensive to run than horse-drawn carriages.

One of Trevithick's early steam-powered locomotives.

STEAM POWER

Coal supply

Coal is burned in the firebox. The heat from the fire passes along tubes that run through a water-filled boiler, heating the water. The hot water boils, producing steam that is fed into pistons. Pressure from the steam pushes the pistons back and forth, and this turns the locomotive's wheels. Smoke from the fire leaves the locomotive through a funnel on top.

ACCIDENTS 👉

Early locomotive accidents were caused by a lack of knowledge of how to handle high-pressure steam. Boiler explosions were common, so locomotives were fitted with safety features, such as a gauge in the driver's cab to monitor pressure and safety valves to release excess steam.

This train has been wrecked by a boiler explosion.

The first intercity link between Stockton and Darlington, UK, was just 40 km long.

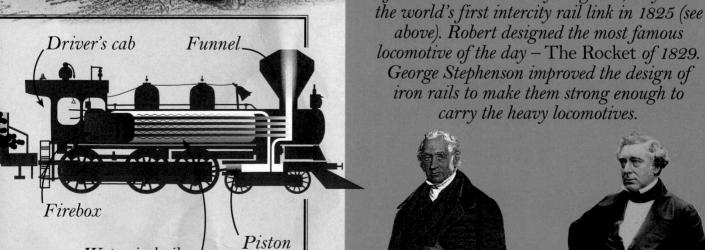

Driver's cab   Funnel

Firebox

Water in boiler   Piston

THE STEPHENSONS

George Stephenson was an English engineer known as the 'father of railways'. His son Robert was one of the most talented engineers of the nineteenth century. Together, they built the world's first intercity rail link in 1825 (see above). Robert designed the most famous locomotive of the day – The Rocket of 1829. George Stephenson improved the design of iron rails to make them strong enough to carry the heavy locomotives.

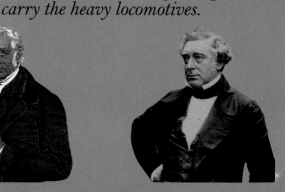

George Stephenson   *Robert Stephenson*

✺ TRAIN ✺
EVOLUTION

As demand for train transport increased, so locomotive design changed to make trains faster, more efficient and more economical.

CROSSING AMERICA 👉

The first train track to cross the whole of the USA was completed in May 1869, when tracks from east and west joined at Promontory Summit, Utah. Completion of the network opened access to the west as steam trains carried more and more settlers to new farm lands.

Locomotives such as this one were used to pull trains across the USA in the second half of the nineteenth century.

HIGH-SPEED STEAM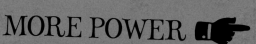

With demand for quicker passenger services between towns and cities, engineers looked for ways to make locomotives faster. One solution was to produce streamlined body shapes, as found on *Mallard*.

Mallard set a world record speed for a steam locomotive of 200 kph in 1938.

MORE POWER

Freight train operators wanted more powerful locomotives to pull bigger trains. Operating from 1941 until 1959, the Union Pacific Big Boy was one of the biggest steam locomotives built. After the Second World War, the increase in coal prices drove the Big Boys out of business, and they were replaced with diesel locomotives.

DIESEL POWER

The first diesel locomotives were built in the early 1900s. They used internal combustion engines (see pages 4–5) fuelled by diesel. They have many advantages over steam locomotives. While steam locomotives take a long time to get started, diesels can be started almost immediately. They can also be operated by a single person, while steam locomotives need a small team to drive them.

Four diesel locomotives pulling a train in the USA.

SPEEDY TRAINS

Designers have always looked for ways to make trains go faster and more efficiently, reducing travel times for people and cargo.

TEST TRAINS

Introduced in the 1920s, the speed kings of the tracks are experimental rocket sleds that run on rails. However, the Opel Rak of 1928 was not a success. It blasted to a speed of about 270 kph, but on its next run, jumped off the tracks and crashed. Rocket sleds are still used today for high-speed tests on ejection seats, missile parts and even people.

In a rocket sled test of 1954, US airman John Stapp tests the effects of rapid deceleration.

STREAMLINING 👉

Built in 1935 in the USA, the *Flying Yankee* dispensed with a steam engine and heavy iron bodywork. Instead it had a diesel locomotive and an aerodynamic body made of lightweight stainless steel. It also had air conditioning in all carriages, which made it hugely popular.

These streamlined trains from the 1930s had a top speed of more than 180 kph.

FLYING YANKEE

TILTING TRAINS

Most trains need to slow down to travel safely around bends in the track. One way of overcoming this is to tilt the train as it moves around a bend. Tilting trains are fitted with hydraulic mechanisms that tilt the train so it leans into the curve. Modern tilting trains are able to travel at speeds of up to 270 kph on curves.

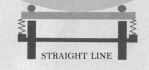

STRAIGHT LINE

CORNERING

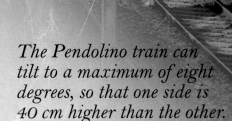

The Pendolino train can tilt to a maximum of eight degrees, so that one side is 40 cm higher than the other.

RECORD HOLDER 👉

The Train à Grande Vitesse (TGV) is a fast French train system introduced in 1981. It uses powerful electric locomotives that take their power from overhead lines and run on specially designed tracks. These tracks are continuously welded to reduce vibrations. They don't have steep slopes or tight bends, so that trains maintain a high speed.

The Thalys TGV operates between Paris, Brussels and Cologne.

UNDERGROUND TRAINS

The need to move people around cities led to the creation of underground metro systems. Since the first opened in London in 1863, many of the world's capitals have built a metro.

THE FIRST METRO

The first underground trains were pulled by steam locomotives, but these filled stations with smoke and made journeys unpleasant for travellers. Engineers tried to minimise the discomfort by building smoke vents and even using a smokeless fuel. By 1900, however, the steam locomotives were all replaced with cleaner electric models.

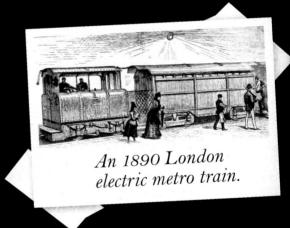

An 1890 London electric metro train.

This 'smokeless' London metro test train of 1862 heated steam with hot bricks. It nearly exploded and never went into service, causing such shame to its designer, John Fowler, that for years he denied it was his.

WORKING ON AIR

The first rapid underground train in New York City was a small service that used compressed air to blow a carriage along a tunnel. Completed in 1870, it was something of a novelty and of little practical use as only one carriage ran at a time. A huge blizzard in 1888 convinced city authorities of the need for a proper subway network. The construction of today's New York Subway began in 1900.

MODERN UNDERGROUND

Some of today's most modern metro systems are in cities that have never had a metro before. The Dubai Metro in the United Arab Emirates opened in 2009 and is the largest driverless, computer-controlled network in the world. Almost half a million people use it every day, but just ten people work in its control room. Human intervention is only needed in the event of a system fault or an emergency.

Dubai Metro trains are driverless.

TRAINS OF THE FUTURE

The trains of tomorrow will be faster and more comfortable than ever before, zooming along at hundreds of kilometres an hour using tracks that won't even have rails.

FLOATING ON MAGNETS

Using magnets to keep the train floating above the track, maglev trains (short for magnetic levitation) are super-fast and can zoom along at 600 kph. By floating, maglevs reduce friction, making it easier to travel fast. The first passenger maglev opened in Germany in 1979, but maglev lines are very expensive to build. Engineers are looking for ways to make them cheaper.

A maglev train being tested in Japan.

A maglev train in Shanghai, China.

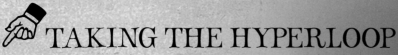TAKING THE HYPERLOOP

The hyperloop is an experimental idea for a transport network using carriages that zoom along tubes at speeds of up to 1,200 kph. These tubes lie below ground or high above the surface, supported on pylons. It is being tested at a small track in California, USA.

Hyperloop carriages would travel through sealed tubes.

MAGLEV

Set into the maglev track are powerful electromagnets that create a strong magnetic field. This repels the magnetic field on the underside of the train, pushing it up so that the whole train floats 1–10 cm above the track. Magnets in the sides of the track then quickly switch their attraction, and this pushes and pulls the train forwards.

Magnets in the train and track keep the train floating above the track.

30

31

INDEX